MARTIAL ARTS
FOR
PEOPLE WITH DISABILITIES

To Deborah,

With all my best wishes in the Martial Arts,

Dick Robert

April 1992.

HUMAN HORIZONS SERIES

MARTIAL ARTS FOR PEOPLE WITH DISABILITIES

An Introduction

DIRK ROBERTSON

A CONDOR BOOK
SOUVENIR PRESS (E&A) LTD

First published 1991 by Souvenir Press (Educational & Academic) Ltd, 43 Great Russell Street, London WC1B 3PA and simultaneously in Canada

ISBN 0 285 63045 8

Photoset and printed at Redwood Press Limited, Melksham, Wiltshire

To
Mum and Dad, Daphne, Deirdre and Lydia,
all family in their own way and to whom
I owe so much

FOREWORD

Seven or eight years ago, if you had told me that people with disabilities or learning difficulties were practising martial arts, I would have found it hard to comprehend — until, that is, I witnessed the author of this book taking a Karate class for people with no lower body mobility whatsoever.

It was at that point that I realised what a blinkered view I had of martial arts in general. Although many Karate instructors lecture that mental development is as important as

Aidan Trimble

physical, it is usually the case that we don't practise what we preach. Dirk Robertson is not one of those instructors. He has done what every good instructor should demand of his student — that is, to improve on his or her achievements. Although he has not won international titles, through his work with people with disabilities and learning difficulties he has surpassed my achievements by improving the lives of many, thus embodying the true meaning of Karate-Do: using it not just as a method of fighting but as an aid to improving the quality of life.

This book covers most disabilities and shows how the martial arts can be adapted to suit particular disabilities, especially in the use of Kata. The author has used some of the most advanced Kata, such as Kanku-Dai and Unsu, as well as covering some of the more internal martial arts such as Tai-Chi-Chuan. However, one of the greatest contributions this book makes is that in addition to welcoming people with disabilities into an activity long considered to be the domain only of able-bodied people, it also enables able-bodied people to take the opportunity to look at the art and themselves in a new and completely different way, and as such I wholeheartedly recommend this book.

AIDAN TRIMBLE, *Fifth Dan*
Former British, European and World Champion,
co-author of *The Advanced Karate Manual* and *Karate Kata* volumes 1 to 4,
Nottinghamshire Karate Coach and Development Officer,
Chairman and Chief Instructor to the Federation of Shotokan Karate.

PUBLISHER'S NOTE

Throughout this book it has been stressed that care should be taken not to exceed the body's capabilities when practising the Kata and forms. The author and publishers are not responsible in any manner for any injury which may occur by reading and/or following any instruction or suggestion in this book. It is essential that medical advice be sought prior to undertaking any of the activities described.

CONTENTS

PART FIVE: MIND AND SPIRIT

ACKNOWLEDGEMENTS

My thanks for advice and support over the years to Aidan Trimble and Vince Morris, and to Paul Warren, Daniel Austen and many others — they know who they are.

For the use of photographs I am grateful to Roy Victor, Roy Dixon, David Bruce, Terry O'Neill of *Fighting Arts International* and Paul Clifton of *Combat Magazine*.

Thank you to John Davey for the drawings which illustrate the Kata and forms described in the text.

I am grateful to the following for permission to quote from published material: Random Century for *The Karate-Do Manual* by P. M. V. Morris, and for *The Three Pillars of Zen: Teaching, Practice and Enlightenment*, edited by D. Kapleau, both published by Hutchinson; Paul Hooley Associates for *Advanced Shotokan Karate Kata* by John Van Weenan.

On the uphill struggle
don't give up, just
push harder and you'll
get there in the end

When everything threatens
to tear your soul apart,
breathe out, clear your mind
and find strength through heart

Dirk Robertson
London 1990

INTRODUCTION

This book is an introduction for people who lead their lives with a disability, of whatever nature, and who may not have considered learning a martial art before, or who may be unsure about the possible benefits in relation to their particular disability or life situation. It is also aimed at instructors and coaches who know that martial arts are for all, regardless of an individual's physical or mental capacity. It is not meant to be a comprehensive analysis of all the martial arts, or their origins. It is not, nor can any book be, an absolute alternative to a competent and qualified instructor.

It takes courage and determination to enter an area of activity about which one knows absolutely nothing — even more so if one has a disability and may be further inhibited by fears of rejection born of ignorance — but in the field of martial arts there is so much waiting for people with disabilities. There is also a tremendous amount of learning to be done by able-bodied people, many of whom who do not realise that they are surrounded by true exponents of the fighting spirit — people with disabilities.

To give you, the reader, an idea of how I first became involved in instructing people with disabilities in Karate, let me tell you how it all began. I am a Black Belt instructor, based in London, and am a member of the Federation of Shotokan Karate. This association is headed by Aidan Trimble, the former World Champion. I have been involved in Karate since I moved to England from my native Edinburgh in 1977.

I first started teaching Karate to people with disabilities when I was at college, training for my professional social work qualification. As part of my practical work I was assigned, one day a week, to a home where there lived a large number of people with disabilities. I was supposed to 'run a group', giving the members some kind of physical or mental activity. Instead of opting for group discussions or repetitive and patronising manual tasks, I introduced the members of the group to movements from Karate.

What struck me most when I first came to the home was the way people's physical condition appeared to govern the way they felt — both spiritually and emotionally. Because they had a disability they tended to think that one would not be interested in them; they appeared to have no sense of self-value. This does not apply to all people with disabilities, but society puts such emphasis on appearance and physical competence that one can easily be made to feel 'second class', just because one has some kind of disability.

Quite early on I met a man who had both a disability and learning difficulties. He stopped me in the corridor one day and said he had trouble running. He said that, when he ran, he fell over and people laughed at him, and that what upset him was not the fact that he could not run, but that people laughed at him. So I asked him not to run, but to show me how he walked. When he walked down the corridor, I noticed that he put his toe down before his heel, instead of his heel before his toe, so that he walked with a

15

'bang'. This altered his spinal position and generally made movement very difficult for him.

I asked him to put his heel down before his toe so that he would find walking easier. He did that straight away and I only had to show him once. Then, when he walked up the corridor he walked normally; he no longer slouched, although his appearance was still a little unusual as the buttons on his shirt were done up incorrectly (which makes another point: the way you dress unfortunately appears to influence the way you are accepted). When he walked properly his mouth remained closed and his tongue did not hang out, which allowed him to speak more comprehensibly. Before this, his slurred and incoherent speech had been attributed to his disability; in fact it was simply because his tongue had been sticking out between his teeth. He had let himself go physically because he did not feel he was important.

It was this realisation that prompted me to start a group, which initially just dealt with physical movements and the way these relate to one's internal harmony and spiritual feeling. I have found that through Karate I have become more co-ordinated both physically and mentally. Often you can concentrate to a very high degree mentally but physically you feel indifferent, whereas the more in tune you become, in mind and body, the more balanced you are with your immediate environment.

16

If you become disabled at any time of your life, or if you have always had a disability, nobody really blames you for choosing to opt out and just let go — not washing your clothes, not bothering about what you are doing, or letting other people take over — not only because of your physical condition but because of your emotional state. Seemingly little things can become very important. The fact you cannot raise your own cup to your lips, or always have to wait for other people to help you in everyday tasks, can and often does rob you of your dignity. That you actually have to ask permission to do these things because other people have a routine as well and you have to fit into that — all this is very emotionally destructive. Thus it is simple to see how the mind becomes cluttered and 'clustered' with problems.

If you are able-bodied and have achieved the ability to relax, then you have attained something well worth having. In the case of my very first group, people with disabilities and with low self-esteem gained, through the practice of Karate, the ability to perceive themselves as unique individuals and were able to relax in the face of seemingly insurmountable problems. This is the main point: you must try and see problems as being smaller than yourself, not greater. The more you give in, the harder it is to get into the frame of mind that you are controlling your problems, they are not controlling you!

I have always found it a moving experience to watch people trying really hard to grow and develop and come gradually to understand the connection between meditation, awareness and the physical movements of Karate and other martial arts. This was especially true of the first group I led, which had about twenty people in it and included individuals with cerebral palsy, Parkinson's, muscular dystrophy, atrophy, polio, multiple sclerosis and many other conditions which they had lived with from birth or had developed later in life. Many were confined to wheelchairs and most had only slight mobility in their upper bodies or limbs.

The main question I asked myself in the early days was, are these movements from Karate any use to people with disabilities? The answer was always yes. Even with only limited movement people can develop a greater level of concentration, self-esteem and personal awareness, as well as physical control over their own lives. The physical movements from Karate and other martial arts are of great relevance as they can develop the muscle control and co-ordination necessary for everyday tasks such as pouring a cup of tea or buttering a piece of toast, or managing personal hygiene.

Since 1981 I have worked, and learned, with a wide range of people with disabilities throughout the United Kingdom and abroad, utilising Karate movements for their particular sets of circumstances. The group of people I started with had severe disabilities and we concentrated on slight movements and the spiritual aspects of the martial arts. Many of the people I became involved with lived in institutions, and their self-image was very low. The practice of Karate was designed to tackle those feelings and the stress of having other people in control of their lives. Over the years I have been approached to instruct groups of people whose disabilities are less and less severe and whose spirits are well developed and strong. These people do not need to be taught how to raise their self-image, but they can benefit in other ways from the physical movements and the spiritual message of Karate and the whole spectrum of the martial arts.

1987 was a very important milestone for me: I won a national award, sponsored by the social work profession and a national magazine, recognising the idea of making Karate accessible to people with disabilities. That my work should be acknowledged at national level was exciting enough, in view of the widespread suspicion that the martial arts are only for hooligans and thugs. What made it really special was the fact that the professional scene accepted the benefits of this type of activity for people with disabilities and thus recognised their right to choose whatever activity they wished to involve themselves in.

That award drew attention to the fact that people with disabilities can and do achieve excellence in exactly the same way as able-bodied people — through sheer hard work and perseverance. It gave what I was doing a kind of respectability, and people from all over the United Kingdom contacted me to express an interest in the involvement of people with disabilities in the martial arts.

In practising Karate I have experienced competition at a variety of levels and have always considered it important to put myself on the line, and under pressure. If one is learning a martial art it is very easy just to train and avoid pressure and face-to-face confrontation. Personally I have never felt comfortable in Karate competition; I have found the stress levels very intense although the overall experience is useful. The reasons for this have very little to do with worrying about physical injury (although in the fighting sections this is always a possibility); they are more to do with concern about letting myself or other people down by a poor performance.

I have competed, in the Kata (movements), in international events in the United States and Europe. I have always found it hard to perform well, but again, just because the competitions were hard does not mean they were of no use. It was the same when I used to enter the fighting sections. One learns that it is not really a game, even in those events termed as sport. For me there is a link between the pressure of competition and life with a disability. Both can be a constant struggle, often without support, and you have to overcome adversity and other people's attitudes and ultimately lead your life as you wish to, not as other people would like you to. Competition Karate and Karate in general, for me, are akin to leading life with a disability in that the real success is gained, before you even begin to perform or 'achieve', if you are able to overcome external pressure and quite literally be yourself.

Part one

BEFORE YOU START

THE MARTIAL ARTS AND THEIR HISTORY

There are as many different types of martial arts as there are disabilities. Some have their origins in China, some in Japan, whilst others hail from Indonesia, the Philippines or South America. Some are relatively modern, developed by students of students, whilst others date back to fighting systems centuries old.

It is important to understand that the practice of a martial art is geared to the development of the mind, character and spirit, and to the harmony of the body with all these essential elements. All you need is to possess these ingredients. Contrary to popular opinion, you do not need a whole and superbly fit body — just a body will do.

All the martial arts have as their central aim the maximising of potential on the part of an individual. They are not aimed at comparing one's own performance or ability with others'. Certain aspects of selected martial arts have been streamlined and developed as a competitive sport from which the participants gain much satisfaction, but they represent only a tiny fraction of the practising martial artists in the United Kingdom and throughout the world today.

The martial scene in general is thought to have been set by a sixth-century Indian monk known as Bodhidharma, who settled in China. He is believed to have lived in a monastery called Shao-Lin and there to have created a fighting system aimed at helping the monks protect themselves (in quite violent times), as well as providing them with an effective form of exercise.

TAI-CHI

There are many different schools of opinion about the origin of Tai-Chi-Chuan, as it is known. It is basically a set of movements with the emphasis on physical and mental development leading to spiritual harmony. Exponents consider it an 'internal' activity, meaning that it relies not on external strength but on inner flexibility. People often confuse this with being passive, which is not the aim: rather, the sets of slowly-performed movements concentrate on non-aggression. They are quite different from the 'external', explosive movements of many other martial forms.

The main principles of Tai-Chi-Chuan are said to be based on a Chinese book known as the *I Ching* (Book of Changes). No one seems to know its exact age, but Confucius (600 BC) is believed to have drawn on it when developing his particular brand of philosophy and approach to life. Taoism, a form of Eastern philosophy, also contributes to the make-up of Tai-Chi-Chuan, with a famous work known as the *Tao Te Ching* (by Lao Tze, a Chinese philosopher), considered by many Tai-Chi-Chuan exponents to be one of the most important Chinese language books ever written. The Chinese have always placed great

21

importance on health and a peaceful mind, and many sets of movements were developed to achieve this, rather than as an efficient means of self-defence.

Tai-Chi-Chuan itself is thought to have been the brainchild of a certain Chang San-Feng, a Taoist monk who lived at some time between the twelfth and fourteenth centuries. He had his monastery on a mountain known as Wu-Tang, and it was there that he developed his system, derived from what he considered the most effective martial forms, combined with breathing forms based on Taoist principles and the philosophical teachings of the *I Ching*.

The main difference between Tai-Chi-Chuan and the other martial forms, which have their historical development more closely connected with Bodhidharma and his Shao-Lin monastery, is that Tai-Chi-Chuan is considered a 'soft' form whilst the others are regarded as 'hard', due to their more aggressive movements and approach.

WUSHU

Many believe that Wushu is the correct name for 'Kung-Fu', which actually started life as 'Gung-Fu'. Kung-Fu was the art popularised by the martial artist and film actor, Bruce Lee. It is a Chinese form incorporating acrobatics with a fine and well-balanced martial attitude and is widely practised by women — indeed, the British Wushu Team is pushing the Chinese for world dominance in this sporting field. Bruce Lee was credited with first having the idea for 'Kung-Fu', the American television serial of the 1970s which made a star of David Carradine.

JUDO

Professor Jigoro Kano was the originator of Judo, which basically means the 'gentle way' and relates to the skill of deflecting an attacker's strength and using it against him in a series of throws and body movements. It is best known as a sport but has deep traditional roots, and its 'Kata' are 'fundamental forms' allowing the practitioner to practise and hone his or her skills.

Great Britain has an excellent world-beating squad who took home 16 medals from the 1990 Commonwealth Games.

TAEKWONDO

Taekwondo means 'way of the foot and fist'. This name was created in 1955 for a Korean martial art. At the conclusion of the Second World War Korea had five main schools catering for the martial arts, known as Mooduk, Jido, Changmu, Chungdo and Songmu. From these there derived a variety of groups and associations, each with its own emphasis on tradition or competition. Taekwondo is well known for its spectacular high kicks, with jumps and turns providing speed and momentum. Its practitioners also promote the art of breaking various objects such as wood and concrete to demonstrate power and timing — indeed, competitions are held which often have breaking techniques as their main feature.

AIKIDO

In common with the other martial arts, Aikido is beset by differences of opinion about who developed what. These arguments can become quite vicious and bitter, but it is generally agreed that Morehei Uyeshiba was an originator and founder of Aikido. Ai and Ki are two separate things and Aiki-do basically means the 'way of mind and body', or 'spirit and body' depending on which way you look at it. Its moves are swift and graceful and wrist and arm locks are in abundance throughout the system, as are formal 'Kata' which are sets of prescribed exercises. The technique is to go with a force and to turn it on itself both physically and spiritually. There is far less kicking and punching in this style than in many others, but this does not detract from its usefulness and effectiveness both as a traditional martial form and as a form of self-defence.

KENDO

The 'way of the sword' is an activity practised to this day throughout the world. The swords used in competition are not real but are designed to allow the participants to score 'points' against specific parts of the body. Armour, usually bamboo, is worn and strict attention is paid to etiquette and tradition. Another aspect is Iaido which, simply put, relates to the art of drawing a sword, and in this case a real sword, known as a 'live' blade, is used. It is the sword, believed to be the soul of the Samurai (feudal period Japanese warrior), which best encapsulates the spirit of Budo or Bushido — the way of the warrior.

An interesting point is that, in competition Kendo, the striking areas are usually the head and upper body, so really there is no reason why this activity cannot be developed usefully for people with disabilities.

KARATE

Karate originated in China, where martial forms were practised by the monks of various temples. Trading and piracy completed a link with the island of Okinawa, off mainland Japan, which in 1372 came under the feudal control of China. This resulted in a more formal exchange of culture and life-styles, and the people of Okinawa began to develop their own form of martial art.

In 1609 Japan in turn defeated and occupied Okinawa and subjected it to the rule of Japanese warlords. This prompted the Okinawans to concentrate even more on their development of the martial arts, in order to defend themselves against the occupiers.

The year 1669 saw weapons and the practice of martial arts banned by the Japanese, which resulted in the Okinawans practising in secret, in order to perfect their techniques. This was the start of the development of recognisable systems and styles. After further periods of unrest through subsequent centuries, Karate was introduced to Japan in 1902 by the efforts of Gichin Funakoshi, the originator of the Shotokan style or 'school' of Karate. He organised a set of demonstrations which so impressed the Japanese that they decided to allow the practice of Karate on the mainland. 'Shoto' was the pen name of Funakoshi, which to this day is represented by the image of a tiger.

Karate is split into three elements — Kata, Kumite and Kihon. Kumite is prearranged and free-flowing fighting between opponents and Kihon are the basic techniques practised in a repetitive manner. It is the Kata, set series of movements each with a different emphasis on speed, power or breathing, which can be practised to great effect by people with a wide range of disabilities and learning difficulties, alone or in a group. You do not need a partner to practise. Kata and forms encapsulate the principles and striving for personal development which are the foundation of traditional martial arts. Because of the disfavour with which the martial arts were regarded by the ruling authorities for so many years, the original Kata were practised with movements which allowed the exponent to carry on for long periods without tuition. The defence movements were usually designed to ward off more than one attacker, so they involved constant changes of direction and emphasis.

Karate, loosely translated, means 'empty hand' and is the practice of techniques related to defence, attack and the deflection of physical aggression. Traditionally the art is known as Karate-Do, 'Do' meaning 'way' and encapsulating the spirit, respect for life and the social responsibility of training with other people. Thus the 'way of Karate' is meant to mean much more than just physical movements: it is an esoteric principle and an attitude to life. The practice of Karate involves 'Kata' of varying degrees of difficulty.

There are many different styles of Karate, all related to the five major schools:

Wado-Ryu
Founded by H. Otsuka in 1939, it means 'way of peace' and lays great emphasis on speed in the techniques generating power. Soft, flowing movements, with an emphasis on balance and timing, are the trademark of this style. The leg stances, which vary from style to style, are middle range in height, allowing swift movements ideal for fast competition.

Shukokai
This means a 'way for all' and was developed by Chojiro Tani. It is a style which adopts a high stance in movement, and is ideal for competition fighting. It lays emphasis on speed of movement rather than power.

Goju-Ryu
This style combines Okinawan and Chinese techniques and was the brainchild of Chojun Miyagi (no relation to the character in *Karate Kid*!). This style has excellent Kata and techniques with an emphasis on strengthening the body.

Kyokushinkai
This means the 'ultimate truth' and was founded by Masutatsu Oyama who placed great emphasis on the spirit and traditional elements of Karate. His style reflects this, with a high profile being given to Tameshiwara, which is the breaking of objects such as wood, to demonstrate and test internal power.

Shotokan

This is the style from which the Kata in this book originate. It lays emphasis on deep, diaphragmatic breathing and rhythmic movement. The Kata are varied and interesting, with a strong concentration on spirit and application of technique.

In common with most of the martial arts, the Karate system has gradings, whereby exponents are tested on their ability, performance of technique, spirit and the forms or Kata. Generally speaking, the first grade for which one can be examined is Ninth Kyu, then, usually three months later (by which time one is expected to have improved), Eighth Kyu, and so on right up to First Kyu. The passing of grades is marked by the wearing of coloured belts:

Ninth Kyu	White Belt
Eighth Kyu	White Belt
Seventh Kyu	Yellow Belt
Sixth Kyu	Green Belt
Fifth Kyu	Purple Belt
Fourth Kyu	Purple Belt with one stripe
Third Kyu	Brown Belt
Second Kyu	Brown Belt
First Kyu	Brown Belt
First Dan	Black Belt
Second Dan	Black Belt
Third Dan	Black Belt

Fourth Dan	
Fifth Dan	
Sixth Dan	all Black Belt, although some wear a Red Belt
Seventh Dan	
Eighth Dan	
Ninth Dan	

The timing from First Kyu to First Dan Black Belt is usually six months, from First Dan to Second Dan two years, from Second Dan to Third Dan three years, and so on. One grades to Third Dan, then it is usual for the other grades to be awarded for service to the art. Grading panels traditionally consist of senior practitioners of the martial arts. Kyu, in essence, means 'boy' or junior, and Dan means 'man' or senior in Japanese.

*   *   *

There is a great divergence of opinion within the martial arts. Many people feel that their emergence as a sporting activity detracts from their traditional purpose as a system for character development and self-preservation. Others argue that to ignore sporting opportunities is to doom the martial arts to continued misunderstanding and mistrust on the part of the media and the general public. In addition, many Western exponents now feel that there is no more to learn from the Orient and have gone their own way, creating even more bitterness amongst those who feel that loyalty and adherence to the Oriental roots are the only way to preserve the unique nature of the martial arts.

Whatever you believe, it makes for a lively debate and there are good arguments on both sides. I know from my own experience that I have gained much of value from purely traditional training, but equally I have learnt much from the modern schools of thinking and the sporting side. My competition experience has been invaluable to me; I have competed in national and international competitions both in the United Kingdom and abroad, and have found nothing to compare with the realistic pressure of being 'on the line' — nowhere to run to and the opportunity to test your skill with an opponent who will do what *he* wants, not what you want him to do. It is the nearest thing to real fighting pressure that one can experience, for one can and does get hurt. The fighting side of Karate competition involves individual and team events, in which one exponent faces another with one or two referees and four corner judges in attendance, to see the action that the referees might (and invariably do!) miss.

A half point (*wazari*) is usually given for a punch or kick which is controlled and connects with the mid-section or face, a full point (*ippon*) for a superior technique (with control) which may involve a kick to the head, stopping just short of hard contact, or a combination of a sweep and punch or kick which, if not controlled, would have finished the confrontation.

Early competitions were on the one *ippon* basis. Many still are, since groups and individuals feel that this is the most realistic way of conducting affairs. One *ippon* basically means one chance, and if an exponent gets an *ippon* then in real life the match would not have continued. Modern competition argues that one *ippon* means either that the match is over too soon, or that the competitors are fearful of doing anything which may leave them vulnerable to an attack, making for an often extremely boring activity for spectators. Thus the system of three *ippons* has been introduced, requiring much more stamina and fitness and a fuller range of techniques. Arguments still rage on both sides, with some saying that to award three *ippons* is ridiculous as this means three 'killing blows', obviously a contradiction in terms.

Kata or forms are judged quite differently in competitions. The exponent performs his or her set and then four corner judges and a main judge give points (like an ice-dancing competition) for poise, style, co-ordination, interpretation and correctness of movement. Again there is controversy in Kata competition: some people perform spectacular movements which have little or no practical application, in order to impress the judges with suppleness and interpretation; but many others argue that the Kata is primarily a set of *practical* moves which must have a realistic interpretation to be functional and relevant to the practice of the martial arts. This is a view to which I subscribe, although watching some competitions where people do moves which are impractical but spectacular is still very entertaining.

One of the main differences between the performances of Kata and Kumite (fighting), both in training and in competition, is that fast-moving, free-flowing fighting really is the preserve of the younger exponent, whereas Kata has no age or (in my opinion) physical limits. The present World Champion at Kata is over 40 years of age and looks set to keep going for a long time yet.

During ten years of teaching the Kata from the Shotokan style of Karate to people with disabilities I have learnt much from watching men and women with different personal and physical obstacles develop and incorporate Kata and forms for their own use and well-being. It is this, more than anything else, which convinces me that you do not have to be fit, well, young or co-ordinated to gain benefit from the martial forms, and you most certainly do not have to be able-bodied to bring something of worth to the martial arts, from which other people can learn. For many exponents, the Kata are the soul of the martial arts and their practice is the key to the deeper understanding of what, on the surface, may appear to be mere sets of movements with no apparent practical use.

PEOPLE WITH DISABILITIES IN THE MARTIAL ARTS

In a wide variety of martial arts there are many fine exponents who have developed their aptitude and skill whilst living their lives with some kind of disability. There are, in fact, far too many to mention in this book, but it is worth looking at a few of them.

BILL WALLACE

Bill Wallace is an internationally known and respected martial artist who overcame a serious disability in his right leg to become the Professional Karate Association Middleweight Champion of the United States, retiring undefeated in 1980.

His right leg was, and is, useless for competitive martial arts, so Wallace just fought left side forward. He learned to use his left leg to compensate for the deficiencies in his right, and developed a reputation for power and precision which has seen him carve a useful career in the movies as a believable 'baddy'. The most interesting thing about Wallace is his refusal to accept other people's assertions, in the early years, that because of his limitation he was incapable of making it in martial arts. He worked on what he knew he could do, not on what others said he couldn't!

CYRIL A. CARTER

Disregarding his disability from childhood, he spent ten years as a competitive gymnast. A qualified coach and widely respected trainer, he has trained Brian Jacks, the former British and European Judo Champion, and was also coach to the *espoir* (young men's) and junior Judo squads of Great Britain.

VINCE MORRIS

A former Chairman of the Martial Arts Commission, he has an extremely serious asthma condition. Despite this he has had a successful career as a competitor, nationally and internationally, and is now the Assistant Chief Instructor of the Federation of Shotokan Karate. He speaks of one aspect of his experience in his book, *The Karate-Do Manual*:

> Every time my teacher would call me out to free-style (fight) with him my heart would sink! I knew what was to come. Sensei* would keep me out, blocking my attacks and showing up my weak defences by the occasional (none-too-gentle) blow, until I began to develop asthma. At this stage, instead of taking pity on my wheezing and gasping, he would begin to

* Sensei: Teacher

Bill Wallace. Photo courtesy of *Combat Magazine*

Vince Morris.

press his attacks until I was almost unable to stand. Still Sensei kept up the pressure, until I could only stagger around, offering a token defence. After a while, I passed beyond all care of life or death, my only remaining thought rapidly assuming importance.

I would not give in!

And only then, as I launched desperate 'do or die' attacks with total commitment, did Sensei call a halt and allow me to drag myself away.

Why? The answer only really came after I myself became a teacher. Sensei was always aware of the possibility of my 'hiding behind' my asthma; making it an excuse for not training as hard as other members of the class, or using it as a psychological balm, to use to soothe my pride, by excusing a poor performance. By continually denying me these indulgences, Sensei made me realise that the powers of *mind and spirit* are always adequate to cope with and overcome limitations imposed by the body. (Incidentally, we never spoke of this after a training session. Only after nine years did Sensei laconically remark: 'Better now, neh?') The student must cultivate the ability to see things in their true perspective, and to be completely honest with himself. This means never making excuses for a bad performance, nor being content with 'coasting along' in training. Eventually, he will be led to understand that it is just as egotistical to be concerned overmuch with defeat as it is to rejoice in victory.*

* *The Karate-Do Manual*, P.M.V. Morris (Hutchinson, 1979).

30

TED VOLLRATH

Ted Vollrath is a Fifth Dan Black Belt Karate exponent. He lost both his legs in Korea in 1953, when the war was at its fiercest. He is constantly in demand throughout his native United States of America for demonstrations and seminars. He is a sterling example of what can be achieved in the face of apparently overwhelming odds.

Ted Vollrath. Photo courtesy of Terry O'Neill, *Fighting Arts International*

THE PRACTICAL BENEFITS OF MARTIAL ARTS

One of the most important benefits of practising Kata is a feeling of self-control, both physical and spiritual. This also extends to the environment — one feels in control of, and at one with, one's immediate surroundings. The examples below illustrate how people with a variety of disabilities have implemented the movements for their own use. Some experienced enormous changes in their situation; for others the effects were less drastic but equally important.

Judy suffers from cerebral palsy. Her condition is extremely severe, and before taking up martial arts she found that conventional physiotherapy brought her little benefit. At night she had difficulty sleeping as her eyes would not close, and for some time she had had a powerful drug administered to enable her to sleep.

The consequence of this medication was that next morning she was unable to concentrate or wake fully alert for the day ahead, never mind the problems of her actual condition. Then she started to practise parts of the Kata Kanku-Dai (see p. 47), both within a group and on her own. Through practice she learned to control her eyes, so that she no longer needed drugs to help her sleep. In the mornings, instead of feeling slow and drowsy, she was now able to participate more fully in life, and she began to challenge the boundaries of the residential home where she lived.

There were many different activities offered in the home, including workshops and drama groups. Judy joined these and her self-confidence continued to grow. She bought attractive clothes to replace the old functional garments which she had worn for the convenience of physical care. Perfume and lipstick followed, and then a relationship with a fellow resident blossomed into a romance.

Foreign holidays, as well as frequent day-trips, became part of her life and it was not long before she moved out of the institution into a home of her own and, equally important, emotional independence. Her physical condition remained unchanged, but the way in which it affected and controlled her life was altered.

How did she form the link between the moves of the Kata and her own needs? Each Kata has a different spiritual and emotional emphasis, and Judy was able to perfect the moves and adapt them for her own needs particularly in relation to breath control. While she performed the Kata she developed a rhythm of breathing which she found comfortable, and this, combined with the movements, allowed her to concentrate her attention on her eyelids. Thus whilst others in her group performed certain moves from the Kata with their limbs, she would attempt to keep her eyes closed for the same length of time. Then, after blinking, she would attempt to keep her eyes closed for a longer period of time, eventually achieving her goal.

* * *

Louise has spent all her adult life in a wheelchair, ostensibly as a result of her physical disability. When I met her she admitted to 'dark' and unhappy times, particularly at night-time. She had only slight movement in part of her upper body, her arms were permanently bent, and her fingers completely curled up. As well as performing *Moksu*, which involves the breathing exercise described on pp. 39–40, she practised the advanced Kata Bassai-Dai, Kanku-Dai and Unsu, with leaps and leg techniques replaced by hand movements. She paid special attention to the spiritual emphasis of the Kata, and took them very much to heart. One day when she was in a hoist, waiting to be bathed, she fell and badly injured herself. Despite this she still came to practise with a smile on her face.

Photo courtesy of Terry O'Neill, *Fighting Arts Interrnational*

'The whole point of practising this stuff is to help me to come to terms with and defeat the problems I encounter,' she said.

The Kata Bassai-Dai is based on the combination of mind and body coming together to 'break down the fortress' of an imaginary adversary and highlights the necessity for good concentration. In this case Louise took the Kata and interpreted her adversary as a combination of her own physical disability and the daily problems which beset her as a direct result of the difficulty of arranging her life to suit other people.

The Kata Kanku-Dai, which underlines the relationship of mind, body and spirit, provided her with a focus as well. The first movements of the Kata require one to bring the hands together in the form of a triangle above and in front of the head. Then one must focus both on the centre and the peripheral elements surrounding it. Louise used this Kata to meditate on her disability — she saw it as being positioned in the centre of the triangle, and the rest of her life and society in general as being the peripheral elements outside the triangle.

In performing this movement one has to focus on everything at the same time, since concentrating too much on the periphery means that what is inside is missed, and concentrating only on the centre disregards the outside elements. Louise saw the same rule applying to her situation: giving too much attention to her own disability (the centre of the triangle) meant that she missed what was going on outside, in every sense of the word. Likewise, if she concentrated overmuch on the outside elements (the periphery), she would be taken unawares by her own perceived limitations connected to her disability.

She felt the Kata Kanku-Dai helped her sense of realism and at the same time strengthened her understanding of the importance of accepting everything as it really was. On the physical side, she developed the ability to open her fingers and fully stretch her arms, so that she can now light her own cigarette and hold and drink cups of tea and coffee. In her own words, she felt that her whole world had opened up and she felt far more in control, both physically and mentally, than she had before.

NOTES ABOUT KATA

In the Shotokan Karate style there are preliminary Kata, known as Heian Kata, and more advanced Kata. The basic and intermediate Kata have an emphasis on blocking and striking. They are enjoyable, useful and dynamic to perform. They also form an excellent foundation for the development of good technique. The Kata which I teach to people with disabilities, however, are in the main advanced ones, not because the basic ones have nothing to offer but because the spiritual and aesthetic principles of the more complex Kata possess much more that is relevant to the life situations of the people I teach, many of whom are living in residential homes. I have therefore concentrated on the more advanced Kata in this book.

The preliminary Kata are as follows:

Heian Shodan
Heian Nidan
Heian Sandan
Heian Yondan
Heian Godan

The words *Shodan*, *Nidan*, *Sandan*, *Yondan* and *Godan* simply mean one, two, three and so on.

The more advanced Kata are:

Tekki Shodan
Bassai-Dai
Chinte
Kanku-Dai
Kanku-Sho
Bassai-Sho
Wankan
Unsu
Jitte
Tekki Nidan
Tekki Sandan
Empi
Nijushiho
Gojushiho-Dai

Karate technique, particularly in the Kata, has very little if anything to do with strength. Helen Raye is neither strong nor tall, but she is one of the foremost Kata exponents in the United Kingdom, winning many times at national and international level. Photo by Roy Dixon

    Gojushiho-Sho
    Jion
    Hangetsu
    Sochin
    Gankaku
    Ji'in
    Meikyō (previously known as Rohai)
    Seienchin

These Kata tend to have varying interpretations and translations of their names, and those that are covered in this book are translated in the sections where the movements are described. Some words, such as *Shodan*, *Nidan* and *Sandan*, have the same meanings as in the Heian Kata. The words *Dai* and *Sho* mean 'greater' and 'lesser' respectively.

    The advanced Kata are not listed in order of difficulty, although some have more complicated moves than others. Kata are not really 'easy' or 'difficult'; awareness, poise, co-ordination and correct attitude are equally important, whether you are performing a more advanced one or not. In fact, many people believe that it is harder for an experienced practitioner to perform a preliminary Kata convincingly than an advanced one. Do not worry if it does not come at first. Keep practising and find the position that is most comfortable for you.

In this book there are many different forms and Kata. Where relevant the spiritual significance is indicated, and if a specific attitude is the aim of the form or Kata, this too is highlighted.

When performing Kata, it is customary to begin and end with a bow — *Rei* in Japanese. This has been described in the instructions for the first Kata, Kanku-Dai (p. 47), but is not repeated throughout the book. If you would like to observe this practice, remember that it should not be a low bow from the waist, but a slight, dignified inclination of the head and upper body to indicate respect.

In some of the Kata, you will find at the end of each movement instructions for breathing in or out and an indication of speed — fast, slow or middle speed. The latter signifies the pace at which the movement should be performed, and the breathing instructions indicate how you should be breathing as you perform the movement.

TERMINOLOGY USED IN THE PERFORMANCE OF KATA

There are various words used to describe attitude and spirit when performing Kata. The following are worth considering if your practice is to develop;

Yoi No Kisin. Preparation, the spirit of readiness.

Tyakugan. The aim and purpose of the Kata.

Inyo. Rather like the Yin and Yang of Tai-Chi-Chuan. In this case it relates to active and inactive.

Waza No Kankyu. Speed appropriate to each technique.

Chikara No Kyojaku. The application of strength and power.

Keitai No Hoji. Positioning.

Zanshin. The most important element. Basically it means awareness, and emphasises the importance of concentrating on what you are doing. It is simply the same level of awareness that people with disabilities exercise every day in their routine tasks.

Kiai. This means the combination of body and spirit (*Ki* and *Ai*) and in the performance of Kata is a shout which is supposed to help to combine the two in a moment of focused energy. If you are able, it also helps to expel air from the abdomen and to tense the body for a split second (see drawing).

Kokyo. Breathing. So crucial to the practice of martial arts that it is covered in detail in the following section. The principle to remember is to breathe in through the nose and out through the mouth.

Tai No Shinshuku. Body positioning in relation to breathing in and out. Expansion and contraction.

Two other words which you will come across frequently are *Jodan* and *Chudan*. These simply mean 'head' and 'stomach' area respectively. *Jodan* is pronounced as it sounds — Joe-Dan — and *Chudan* is pronounced Choo-Dan.

BREATHING — *KOKYO*

It is impossible to overstate the importance of a breathing pattern to gain the maximum possible benefit from the practice of martial forms. What one does not have to worry about is attaining a 'correct' pattern or rhythm, for there is no such thing. Everyone has his or her own personal rhythm and way of breathing, and one should aim to practise in a way that is comfortable and realistic.

The most common way of breathing, particularly for Westerners, is to take their breath in to expand the chest. To achieve a relaxing and efficient breathing pattern it is better to take the air in *through the nose*, down *past* the chest to the stomach diaphragm, then out through the mouth. Where possible, keep the shoulders still and expand the stomach when the air comes in, rather than trying to keep the tummy small and tight as people often think they should.

After a while you will find that the breathing and the movements become as one and you will establish your own unique pattern of breathing. When you start it can help to breathe in and out to a count. Then after a while you lose count and just let go!

If you are dependent on a wheelchair for mobility, commence the breathing pattern without moving your arms, if you have use of either of them. Then, when you feel ready and confident, remove the sides of the chair and concentrate on centring your breathing and balance in the stomach area. The Japanese believe that this is where your *hara* or spirit is confined — hence the ritual suicide called *hara-kiri* when the belly is cut; it is to free the spirit as well as to commit suicide.

. If you have trouble breathing, try doing it to music. Any simple tune that you like will do. If you are distracted initially by what you can see around you, try darkening the room and practise the breathing pattern in complete silence, just listening to the sound of your own breath.

When performing the moves, you focus at the end of each movement. In Karate and other 'external' martial arts this is known as *kime* — focus. It just means that you concentrate, for a split second, as you breathe out and expand the stomach. If you can, tighten your muscles at the same time. It is similar to the concentration you give to the task of opening the lid of a jam jar which is difficult to unscrew.

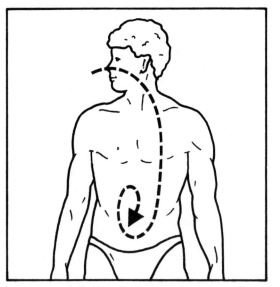

The breathing method is to draw the breath in through the nose and down to the stomach area...

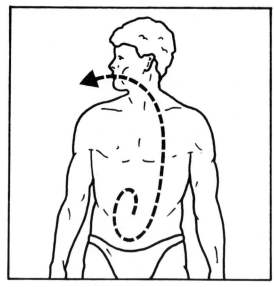

... then out through the mouth.

Usually draw the breath in when you make a movement towards your body...

... and breathe out when you make the movement away.

CALISTHENICS

Before you start practising the Kata described in this book, you should do some preliminary loosening-up exercises to relax your muscles and prepare them for the unaccustomed movements. The book is divided into Kata for those with upper body movement only, for those with lower body movement and for those with full use of their body, so choose the range of exercises appropriate to your own condition.

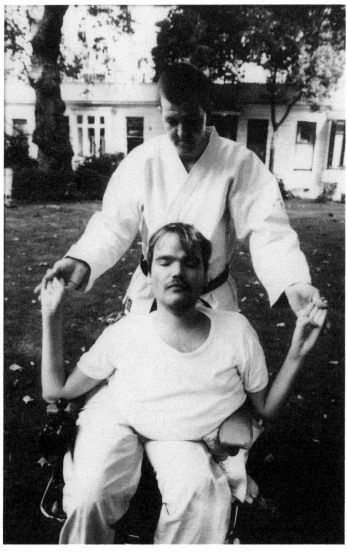

Calisthenics. Photo by David Bruce.

Upper Body

There are many different exercises for loosening off the upper body. It is best to start with the neck and then move on to the shoulders and arms. With your shoulders relaxed, move your head back and forth and then from left to right. Don't forget to breathe evenly, in through the nose and out through the mouth

Next take your left arm and reach up to your right shoulder and grasp your shoulder with your left hand. Use your right hand to push the left arm as far as is comfortable, then repeat on the other side. Manipulate the wrists on both hands by grasping the fingers and moving the hand in a circular motion in both directions. Finally, with your hands by your sides, move both shoulders backwards and forwards until a feeling of loose relaxation is achieved.

Lower Body

Do not hurry stretching exercises on the lower body and legs. Remember that your muscles will stretch in their own good time. Like you, they do not like to be hurried or 'bullied'. So be kind to yourself and, when stretching your legs, simply find a point which starts to pull on your legs and hold it for a short period of time, increasing the duration each time you do it. Do not 'bounce' in order to achieve a longer stretch in your legs, as this rips and tears your muscles and they can take a long time to heal. *Take your time*!

Part Two

UPPER BODY

UPPER LIMBS — STRIKING POINTS

The hands and arms are used in the martial arts, as are the legs, to strike and hit various targets. In the Kata and forms the targets are imaginary — you visualise what you are aiming at. The arrows signify the parts which would make contact with the target.

Uraken — back fist. You make a clenched fist and the arm is usually snapped at the target in a whiplike motion. Remember to keep your elbow in line with the target — if you are able to.

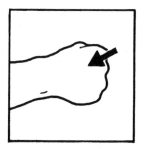

Seiken — fore-fist. The conventional fist with the fingers curled in and covered by the thumb. It is important to keep the balance between tension and relaxation. Don't overtense the hand, but don't keep it too loose either.

Shutō — knife-hand. Tense the fingers together and make sure the thumb is bent a little and presses to the bottom of the first finger.

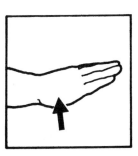

Haitō — ridge-hand. Very similar to *Shutō*, but there is a difference in that the thumb is bent far more and pressed against the palm of the hand rather than the first finger.

Enpi — elbow. The elbow itself is used — again remember to try not to let the elbow drop out of line when you are doing the technique. If you are in a wheelchair and have not removed the arms, be careful to raise your arm *before* you thrust the elbow out, so as to avoid hurting yourself or experiencing unnecessary discomfort.

Ude — forearm. This is mainly a part of the body used for blocking, but sometimes a technique arises which uses it for striking. The forearm-style blocks figure quite substantially in many Kata and forms.

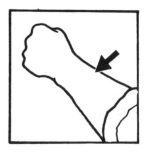

Photo by Dirk Robertson.

46

KANKU-DAI

Kanku basically means 'to look at the sky'. In its complete version it is a long and complicated Kata, involving many jumps and turns. It is supposed to represent the unity of yourself with the heavens and earth.

In all there are 101 movements, beginning and ending with a bow — *Rei* — in common with all Kata. The origin of this Kata is attributed to a Kendo master who brought it to Okinawa, at which time it was known as *Kushanku*. The term 'to look at the sky' relates to the opening movement, in which the hands, with thumbs touching, create a triangle framing the sky above and beyond. One's aim is to view everything without distraction, whilst at the same time accepting what one sees as it really is. The important idea to grasp is the oneness of physical form and seemingly empty air — hence 'look at the sky'.

This Kata was much used by Gichin Funakoshi, the founder of modern Karate, to highlight the versatility and dynamic movements of this style of martial art.

From this Kata there are fourteen moves specifically useful for people with upper body mobility, which I have put together over the years in my classes for people with disabilities.

Begin with a bow.
Placing the hands together, thumbs and fingers touching, hold them out, slightly in front of the body. Breathe in. *Slow*.

Raise the hands above your body and keep the hands together forming a triangle. Pause and focus. Breathe out, then in. *Slow*.

Open the hands, palms facing outwards, and bring the hands in a circular motion back in front of the body. Breathe out, then in. *Slow*.

Bring the edge of the right hand back into the open palm of the open left hand, looking straight ahead, in a smooth flowing movement. Breathe out, then in. *Firm, middle speed*.

Look to your left, bringing your hands to the right hip.
Breathe out, then in. *Slow*.

Block open hand — *Kaishu-Haiwan-Uke*. Breathe out,
then in. *Fast!*

Look to the front, right hand over left. Breathe out, then
in. *Slow*.

Left hand — *Tate Shuto Uke* — pushing block. Breathe
out, then in. *Slow*.

Right *Chudan Zuki* — middle area punch looking straight ahead. Breathe out, then in. *Fast!*

Turn the hips and bring the right hand to the left hip. Breathe out, then in. *Middle speed*.

Block right *Chudan Uchi-Uke* — middle level block. Breathe out, then in. *Middle speed*.

Left *Chudan Zuki* — middle level punch. Breathe out, then in. *Fast!*

Turning the hips, bring the left hand to the right hip.
Breathe out, then in. *Middle speed*.

Block left *Chudan Uchi-Uke* — middle level block.
Breathe out, in, out. *Middle speed*.

Finish and bow. Bow in the fashion most comfortable to you — not a full grovelling bend but a dignified, respectful slight lowering of the head and upper body.

TAI-CHI-CHUAN

Tai-Chi-Chuan relates to the 'hard' and 'soft' elements of life known as Yin and Yang, which also embody the concepts of male and female, night and day, and so on — opposites which together make a whole. The entire philosophy surrounding Tai-Chi-Chuan relates to this aspect of the Chinese attitude to life in general. *Tai-Chi* means 'supreme pole' and *Chuan* is the word for 'martial art'.

The idea of a 'supreme pole' is basically something which holds other things up and allows them to exist and develop. The supporting 'pole' itself does not alter: it is a constant in an ever-changing pattern. This, in simple terms, is the concept of Tai-Chi-Chuan.

The practice of Tai-Chi embodies the idea of attaining a calmness or stillness even if the peripheral elements are stormy. Thus the movements are precise, relatively slow (very slow in some cases) and constantly relate to the 'Yin' and 'Yang' of life. As in many of the other martial arts, there is much debate about the origins and the development of the teaching, and consequently quite a few different styles exist today. However, they all incorporate the same elements of partner work, weapons, and individual forms along the same lines as Kata, although they are executed quite differently from the latter. Between each style of Tai-Chi there is a lot of variation in the forms and in the length of time taken to complete each one. If you go very slowly it can take up to twenty-five minutes in the case of longer forms, compared to the Kata in Japanese Karate, which rarely last more than three to four minutes with the majority taking about one-and-a-half to two minutes.

In contrast to the Karate Kata, there should be complete compliance in the movements, so the joints are not fully locked and the aim is fluid harmony rather than forceful technique. It is important to remember that it is not a case of one martial art being better than the other. It is simply a case of being different.

Chi is the life-force which flows through the body, and it is the flow of *Chi*, and its balance with other elements in the body, which dictate physical and emotional well-being. This idea is intrinsic to Tai-Chi. There are thought to be twelve pairs of *Chi* 'channels' in the body, with a further eight subsidiary ones. When the flow is sweet and balanced everything is in harmony; when the flow is interrupted or hampered in any way, then ill-health and emotional unhappiness are the result. The practice of Tai-Chi helps to preserve the balance of *Chi* in the body and thus maintain physical and mental health.

There are many forms in Tai-Chi-Chuan. The short form given below is suitable for people with upper body mobility. In Tai-Chi-Chuan there are 'long' and 'short' forms, the 'short' forms being abridged versions of the 'long' forms, composed of a series of postures put together to make one continuous movement. This one is from the 'Yang' style of Tai-Chi-Chuan (Yang Cheng Fu was a leading exponent of the art).

While executing these movements, try and think of the hands taking the arms on a journey rather than the other way round, and where possible keep the upper body completely relaxed — enjoy what you are doing. Remember that it does not matter how long it takes you, there is no 'correct' time limit. It takes as long as it takes and your only requirement is to accomplish the form as best you can.

Breathing in, prepare your hands with palms facing back and fingers forward.

Breathe out and lift the arms to chest height, with the hands as limp as possible.

Slowly raise the hands, drawing the breath into your body.

Draw the wrists back towards the body at shoulder height, exhaling evenly.

Drop the wrists, taking the hands down with them as though the wrists are leading the hands, which in effect they are. Breathe in.

Lower the upper body slightly (or as much as is comfortable) and push the hands downwards, palms down, and breathe out.

CHINTE

Chinte is pronounced Chin-Tay and is a very good Kata for people with upper body movement, since its emphasis is on the arms and shoulders rather than on kicking techniques. Whilst this is a Shotokan Karate Kata and as such is Japanese in character, it has its roots firmly in Chinese form. It was originally named *Shoin* by Funakoshi, but this name is not used today.

The circular movements are very good for exercising the shoulders and encouraging co-ordination of hand technique.

There are 35 moves in the complete Kata, reduced here to a sequence of eight.

Kata *Chinte* at the Dutch Open Karate Championships. Photo by Roy Dixon

Place the right fist on top of the left fist with the left fist facing upwards and the right one facing down. This is the *Yoi* position (Ready). Breathe in. *Slow*.

Look to the right and perform *Tettsui Uchi* (bottom fist strike). Breathe out. Bring the arm in front of the face before performing an arc with the arm. *Slow*.

Return the right arm to the original position but this time place it *under* the left fist, facing forward. Breathe in. *Slow*.

Tettsui Uchi, this time to the left. Breathe out. *Slow*.

Awase Shutō Age Uke (double upper rising knife hand block). Turning to the right, bring both arms up from the hips, fingers and thumbs touching. Breathe in. *Fast.*

Looking to the right, if possible (this represents 180° from the original position) perform *Shutō Uke* (vertical knife hand block). Breathe out, then in before performing the next move. *Slow.*

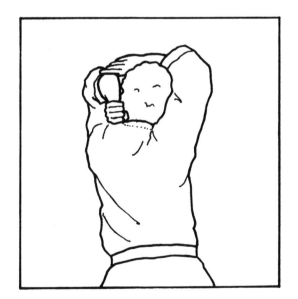

Tate Enpi Uchi (assisted upper elbow strike). *Kiai* — shout (see p. 38). Breathe out, then in. *Fast.*

Looking back to the original position, eyes forward, perform left *Chudan Shutō Uke* (middle level knife hand block). Breathe out. *Middle speed.*

ADVANCED KATA WITH A SPIRITUAL APPLICATION

The following four Kata each have many moves. They are a selection of the advanced ones which I use in teaching people with disabilities and are particularly applicable because of their spiritual application to everyday life. I have not reproduced each Kata in full, but have presented the short sequences of moves which I use when teaching.

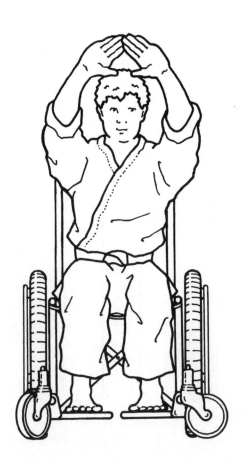

BASSAI-DAI

Bassai means 'to storm a fortress' and highlights the strong spirit of the martial arts. The attitude is one of steadfast concentration and resilience. If any one Kata underlines the philosophy of not giving up, for me it is this one.

    This Kata exists in two forms — *Dai*, the longer one, and *Sho*, the shorter one. The six moves given here are from the longer version which, in its complete form, consists of 52 separate parts. As in all the Kata, the breathing is very important, so concentrate on performing the moves with even timing.

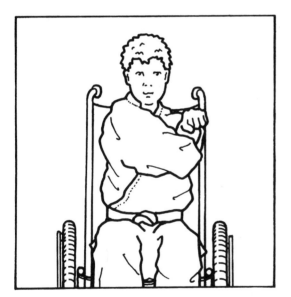 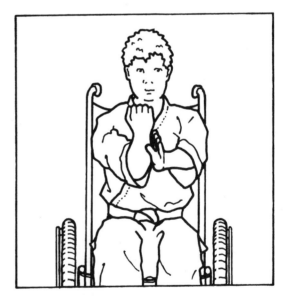

Swinging the right arm from the left shoulder, perform a right hand block pushing the left hand into the right forearm. In a spiritual sense this movement relates to the way one has to be prepared for life's daily demands.

Raise the arms above the head, and breathe in. This is an aggressive and strong movement. Focus on the area in front of you, the way you would focus on problems or difficulties in your life.

Break open the arms and hold them in position, with the chest pushed forward. This movement means that opening the arms is the result of a conscious decision, in the same way that you would tackle a problem.

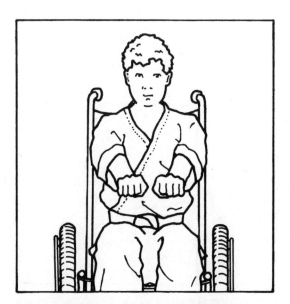

Strike with both fists — middle level strike and thumbs in. There is a time for action, a time to take control, in relation both to life and to its various elements.

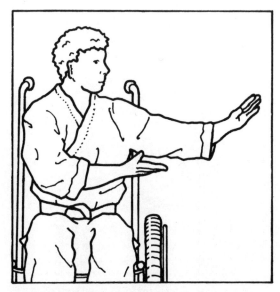

Look to the left, and perform knife hand block — *Kiai*! This is the last movement of the Kata proper, and the last of this sequence. The sense of completion and its relationship to the *Kiai*, and the sense of self-control, are the essential elements.

EMPI

Empi means 'flight of the swallow', and this Kata relates to the movements that a swallow makes in flight. It is unique in that it is performed in a truly open way, with a sense of unguarded moments and a feeling of elation and joy which the movements incorporate and help to develop. This should be a light, relaxed Kata to perform.

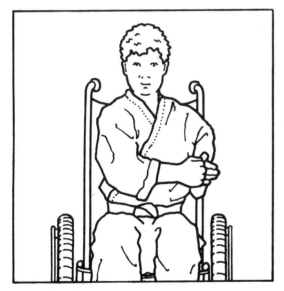

Left open palm at left side, right fist placed against it. Look straight ahead. Preparation is the key element in the Kata — and in life. Being prepared for life's ups and downs also demands flexibility. Life's obstacles can be tackled like swallows in flight — as it comes, go with it.

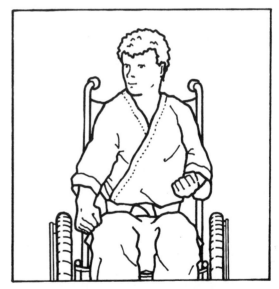

Look 45° to the right and block low with the right hand, left fist to left side. Like the first step of a journey, this movement prepares you for a fluid but firm range of responses intrinsic to a positive quality of life.

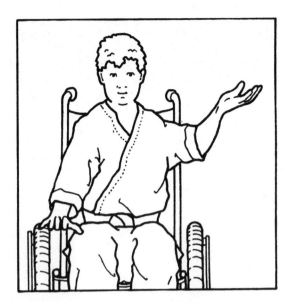 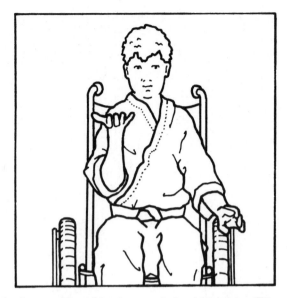

Bringing the hands back as in the left drawing, push the left palm down and the right palm up, as in the right drawing. This movement is the first of three which are linked together. Concentrate on the form of the hands, just as you would face life with poise and dignity.

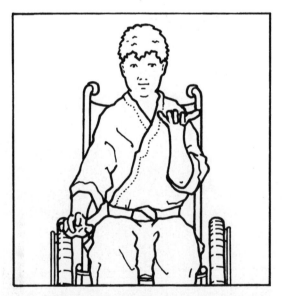 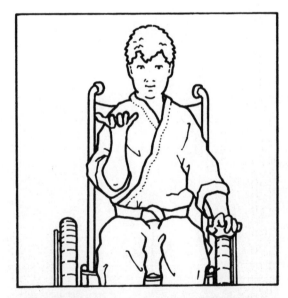

Left open palm pushed upwards, and the right open palm pushed downwards. This is the second of the three movements and is the reverse of the first one. Try to think about a bird spreading its wings, and open your chest by breathing in a balanced way.

Left open palm pushed downwards, and the right open palm pushed upwards, as in the other movements. This final movement of the three requires you to focus all your energy on the arms in front of you, as one must focus on a challenge.

Bassai-Dai.

Empi.

Unsu.

Jitte. Photo by Dirk Robertson

63

UNSU

This is a very old Kata which has seen several changes of name through the years. *Unsu*, meaning 'cloud hands', reflects the way clouds constantly change, although this may not be obvious to the casual observer. The meaning is seen in the movements of the Kata, constantly changing throughout its performance, and in the movement of the hands to push away those of the opponent. The similarity between clouds meeting to create thunder and the hands meeting in confrontation is also worth noting.

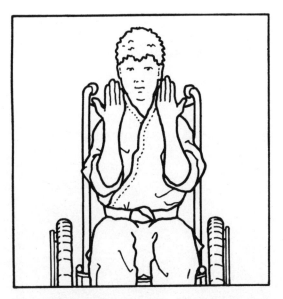

Raise the hands, palms towards you. As the hands meet like thunderclouds, so your body and spirit fuse to reach out and be as one in your life.

Push out, and extend your arms as far as they will comfortably go. Focus on the ground ahead and in front of you. Breathe out as you push out.

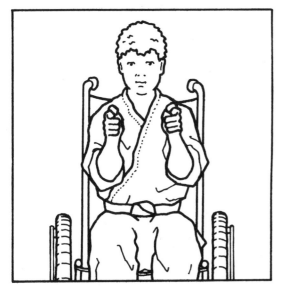

Bringing the arms down and in front of your body, hold the hands as in the drawing, with the thumbs bent and the forefingers straight and pointed. This movement is good fun and unusual to perform. Keep the fingers straight and the arms poised. When I do it I think of jabbing at a problem!

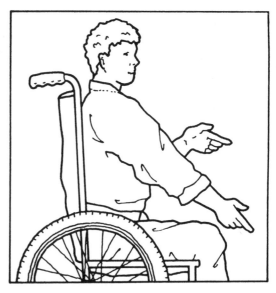

Strike with the right hand, breathing out as you do so. Keep the left hand steady and poised, as in the balance of mind and body. As in the previous move, think of striking at a problem connected with your own life.

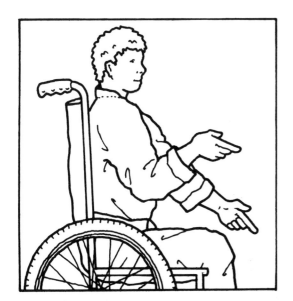

Strike with the left hand, keeping the right one poised and steady — the reverse of the previous movement. Keep poised and balanced.

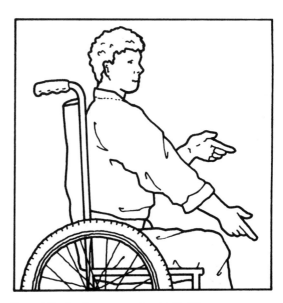

Repeat the fourth movement — and finish.

JITTE

The techniques in this Kata are strong and purposeful. The name (formerly *Jutte*) means 'ten techniques', suggesting rather optimistically that once you have mastered the Kata you could face ten opponents. The complete Kata has only 27 movements and is practised to develop skills of defence against the *bo* (fighting stick). The hand movements, with the palms up and turning, are those of grabbing at a stick.

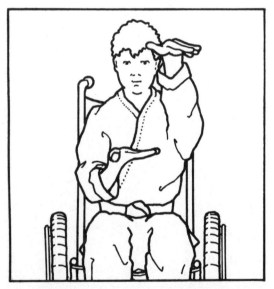 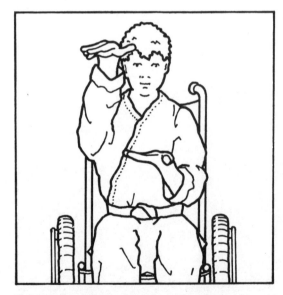

Thrust the hands out, left above, right below, as though grabbing a pole. The movements of this Kata are very popular with the groups I teach. The twisting and turning suggest ways in which you can arrive at the truth about yourself. This is a metaphor developed by my students.

Twist the top and bottom hands, so that the thumbs reverse. This is not difficult — just twist the hands round. The movements should be fluid and precise — with contentment being derived from the precision.

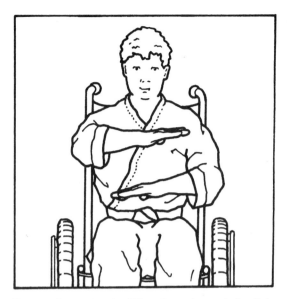

Reverse the arms and pull them towards you. In the Kata proper you twist to the rear, but that is not possible for everyone doing this Kata, particularly those in wheelchairs. Keep your mind concentrated on the task and it will flow.

Looking to your right, raise the left arm and lower the right. When focusing your mind on movements such as these, do not worry if your mind wanders — but always try and remain in control, and in possession of choice.

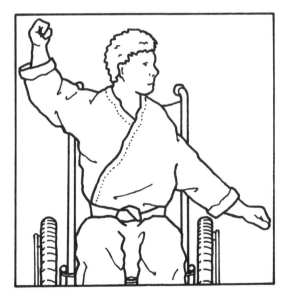

Perform the same movement, but to the left, by twisting the body and arms in the opposite direction. This is the final movement of the set and should be performed with spirit and focus.

Part Three

LOWER BODY

INTRODUCTION

People with disabilities, who have lower body movement, have an extremely wide range of capabilities. Some of you have a limited amount of movement whilst others of you have a full range of lower body movement combined with suppleness and agility.

Find your own level and practise only what you feel comfortable with. In the illustrations the arms have been left in as not all people who do not use their upper body possess no upper limbs.

Balance is a personal thing. Everyone is different, so practise until you find a point of balance which is comfortable for you. For some of the kicks there can be much benefit from having a partner hold you until you are happy doing it alone or even using a chair or a wall for support until you wish to do otherwise.

The breathing is simple in every case: you breathe out on the technique and perform it at a speed comfortable for you. In the kicking section there are advanced kicks and a jumping kick. Do not be put off — this is not for everyone — but I would be doing a disservice to many people with disabilities by not including them, since there are many who, while not using their upper body, are more than capable of performing these techniques. Relax and try to keep your centre of gravity as low as possible. When trying the kicking techniques, do not worry so much about suppleness as about keeping the supporting leg bent, if possible, and turning the heel of the supporting leg towards the direction of the kick. Again, if you can, keep your head turned towards your target, as your head is heavy and can easily overbalance you.

These techniques can be practised by people with visual impairments who have the range of body movement appropriate to lower body techniques.

Photo by Roy Victor

TAI-CHI-CHUAN

Try these three short leg movements from the Yang style of Tai-Chi-Chuan.

Concentrate on the ground beneath you and, if possible, keep the legs relaxed with the toes pointing outwards. Try to get your centre of balance onto your toes and the balls of your feet. Breathe in.

Then breathe out and slowly put most of your weight onto your right foot. At the same time lower the height of your body by bending the right leg and, lifting from the knee, raise the left leg until just the toes are touching the ground with no weight on the left leg. Breathe in, then...

73

Step with the left leg to your left and, breathing out, *place* the foot on the ground and allow your weight to rest on it. With the weight on this leg, now bring the toes of the right leg round to face forward in the same direction as those of the left leg

Repeat this form, going back to the first step each time. Try to avoid speeding up.

KARATE STANCES

These are the positions of the body from which Karate techniques are executed. They are a discipline in themselves and in regular Karate classes are practised on their own without actually performing a technique with the upper body.

The breathing is simple. Remember to breathe in *before* you move and breathe out as you move, focusing at the completion of each technique.

You can put together your own combinations, using those which are most satisfying and appropriate for you to perform.

Hachi ji-Dachi. This is the *natural stance*. You stand with your toes out and heels in, with your feet more or less shoulder-width apart. Try to develop a feeling of relaxed and quiet calm.

Kokutsu-Dachi — back stance. Keep your hips 45° to the front and heels in line, with about 60 to 70 per cent of your weight on your back leg. This is commonly a stance from which defensive moves are executed.

Zenkutsu-Dachi — front stance. Try to keep the feet of both legs pointing in the same direction, if possible, and about 60 per cent of your weight on the front leg. This is a stance which is built for going forward. Keep your back leg straight and relaxed and bend the front leg. A good pointer, again if you are happy doing it, is to keep the knee of your front leg in line over the toes.

Nekoashi-Dachi — cat stance. The best way to describe this is to say that it is a modified example of the back stance. With only ten per cent of the weight on the front leg and the front foot resting on the toes make sure your front knee is turned inwards as a protective measure in case of an attack to your groin. Good for moving around, this one! Give it lots of practice.

Ju-Dachi — freestyle stance. A more mobile adaptation of the front stance, most used in free-flowing fighting. This stance has several variants, some people arguing for a higher stance than others.

Hangetsu-Dachi — half-moon stance. So named because of the shape it makes with the legs. Keep the knees turned inwards and the hips forwards. A satisfying stance to master.

Kiba-Dachi — horse stance. A sideways stance with the legs moving up to one another or crossing over when in motion. Weight is equal on both legs, and remember not to raise your body when moving (if possible).

KARATE KICKS

The kicking techniques are probably the most well-known of the martial arts. They are powerful and spectacular when executed properly and are an excellent exercise for the whole range of muscles in the lower body. It is important to remember that you must find your centre of balance before executing the leg techniques. The head is a very heavy part of the body, so make allowances for its position when kicking. The upper body also plays an important part, so if possible place your upper body as far forward as possible to help your balance. If this is not possible, then one way of compensating is to lower your centre of balance by bending your supporting leg further. Breathe in before the execution of the technique and exhale as you perform the kicking action.

The early Karate techniques only really had the front kick, round kick and side kick in the repertoire, with the emphasis on the lower stomach areas. The flamboyant head kicks were later additions and even today are considered by many purists to be unnecessary and showy. They are, however, a legitimate part of the kicking repertoire. The jumping kick is reputed to have been developed to enable someone to leap up and kick a man off his horse. How accurate this is remains the subject of some debate. When performing this kick, do give some thought to how you are going to land!

Photo by Roy Dixon

MAE-GERI — FRONT KICK

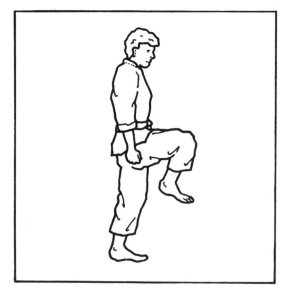

Feet slightly apart.

Raise your leg as high as you can with the foot relaxed. Try to avoid pointing your toes towards the floor.

Then thrust or snap your leg out. Be careful not to raise the foot of your supporting leg as this can overbalance you, and also try and avoid leaning backwards.

MAWASHI-GERI — ROUNDHOUSE KICK

Keeping the leg which is supporting you bent, lift the kicking leg as high as you can. Try to make sure the knee is higher than the foot of the kicking leg so that the movement is fluid and comfortable.

Turn the hips towards the target, keeping the leg up. Make sure the supporting leg is bent, particularly if your limbs are not supple.

Snap the leg towards the target, bringing it back quickly before the knee drops down, and twist your upper body, if you have upper body movement, in order to counterbalance the lower body.

USHIRO-GERI-KEKOMI — THRUSTING BACK KICK

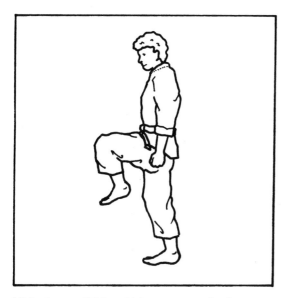

Lift the knee until it is as high as you can raise it.

Then thrust it backwards in a straight line behind you.

When it is thrust as far as you can go, tense your muscles for a split instant to 'hold' the technique.

Do not allow yourself to lean too far forwards as you may overbalance, and also make sure that you do kick straight back to the rear. It is very easy for this kick to go all over the place if you are not careful, so it would be wise not to do this one, or indeed any of the kicks, too near other people until you have achieved some confidence with it.

Kicking against a bag (which can be purchased at any good martial arts shop) is good as it gives you a feeling of what it is like to hit a target, and this helps to improve your technique.

YOKO-GERI KEKOMI — SIDE THRUST KICK

Lift the knee.

Point it in the direction of the target, keeping the supporting leg bent.

Then thrust or snap it out towards the target, pushing the hips.

YOKO-GERI-KEAGE

This is the snap version of the kick Yoko-Geri Kekomi
and is different in that the edge of the foot is pointed at
the target, rather than the sole or the heel, as is the case
in Yoko-Geri Kekomi.

TOBI-GERI — JUMPING KICK

This is an ambitious and spectacular kick which requires
you to push strongly off the back leg, then you perform
the kick of your choice before landing on the ground.
Avoid jumping *at* the target; rather get the distance right,
then jump in the air, performing your technique to the
side.

Part Four

FULL BODY MOBILITY

INTRODUCTION

If you have a wide range of physical movement throughout your body, but have some type of disability such as learning difficulties or problems with sight, then the following selection of forms from Tai-Chi-Chuan will be the type that you can perform. They can be practised alone, or where appropriate if aid is helpful, with a partner in attendance. Again, remember to breathe and to move in a relaxed fashion. Try not to hurry any movement and keep your centre of balance low.

GRASPING THE BIRD'S TAIL

Putting your weight onto your left leg, turn your body to the right and make a semi-circle with your right hands, as though you are painting the floor with an invisible paintbrush.

Now put your weight onto your right leg, bringing your left arm over to join your right.

Step sideways.

Put your weight back onto your left leg, bringing your left hand level with your waist, palm facing down, and bring your right over to join it underneath, palm facing up.

Focus on your right hand and step onto your right foot.

Push up — put all your weight on right leg, right palm up, left one down.

Reverse the palms.

Put your weight back onto your left leg and watch your left hand as it comes back along with your right, level with your waist, placing the palm of your left hand against the right wrist.

Put your weight back onto the right leg.

Take your arms apart, at shoulder height, with palms facing down.

Pull back — bring the weight back onto the left leg, bring your hands back to the middle.

Pointing your fingers up, turn your palms out and push forward, putting your weight onto your right leg.

NEEDLE AT SEA BOTTOM

Kick the left leg out and place your body as in illustration.

Shifting weight to left leg, bring your left hand back, bend it at wrist, keeping your right foot loose.

Bend, keeping your upper body in one straight line, eyes looking at the ground.

FAN THROUGH BACK

Raise your left hand above your forehead and raise your right hand palm facing out. Step forward with right foot.

Shift your weight onto the right leg, push forward with right hand, palm facing out, fingers up.

NOTE: both 'Needle at Sea Bottom' and 'Fan through Back' are reversed from their normal direction. You can vary direction and whether you use your right hand first or your left. It's your choice!

Part Five

MIND AND SPIRIT

ZEN

Zen Buddhism relates to the striving for the ability to accept and realise life and the present for what it really is. It has its roots in the oriental world of Japan and China as well as the Indian continent.

The aim of Zen is to achieve enlightenment, which is known as *Satori*. How this is achieved varies from one school of thought to another. For example, the school of *Rinzai* argues that the intellect of an individual must be developed by the use of *Mondo*. This is the process of questioning and answering between pupil and master:

> One day a man of the people said to the Zen master Ikkyu: 'Master, will you write some maxims of the highest wisdom for me, please?' Ikkyu immediately took his brush and wrote the word 'attention'.
> 'Is that all?' asked the man. 'Will you not add something more?'
> Ikkyu then wrote twice running: 'attention, attention'.
> 'Well!' remarked the man rather irritably, 'I don't really see much depth or subtlety in what you have just written.'
> Then Ikkyu wrote the same word three times running: 'attention, attention, attention'.
> Half-angered, the man demanded: 'What does that word "attention" mean anyway?'
> Ikkyu answered gently: 'Attention means attention.'*

This was the beginning of a *Mondo*, in that the question and answering process appears to have no end until the pupil accepts what is.

Another way to achieve enlightenment is by using a *Koan*, which is a puzzle or idea that intellect alone cannot solve. Grasping the reality is the way forward. Thus we can see that Zen is not something which is there to be written about but something to be experienced. Everyday living is a Zen experience, if one allows it to be, and in itself can be uplifting — even the problems and stressful aspects have their use and place in the total picture. The acceptance of life as it really is remains the ultimate goal in dealing with the stress, pressure and tension allied to both modern living and, more importantly, living with a disability which is either physical, mental, social or a combination of all three.

Another Zen school is that of *Soto* which places great emphasis on meditation by the use of *Zazen*, a means of just sitting and accepting what is. The consideration and grasping of thoughts is not the essential element but more the stilling of the mind, so that thoughts take their relaxed and stress-free place in the order of the conscious and sub-conscious mind.

The place of Zen in the martial arts is in striving for the ability to transcend the intellect when fighting. The major consideration is to be concerned with the here and now, since life itself may depend on it. Moral, ethical and conscious thoughts all serve to clutter the mind and create a situation in which there is little room for flexible reaction.

Zen fighting is the same as zen in living, in that we must learn to react only as the situation arises. This does not mean that you can achieve a good life-style without planning, but flexibility is an essential element.

* *The Three Pillars of Zen: Teaching, Practice and Enlightenment*, ed. D. Kapleau (Hutchinson, 1965).

MEDITATION

A young boy travelled across Japan to the school of a great and famous swordsman. When he arrived at the school he was given an audience with the founder, who was impressed that this young boy had made such a long journey.

'What do you wish from me?' the master asked.

'I wish to be your student and become the finest swordsman in the land,' the boy replied. 'How long must I study?'

'Ten years at least,' the master answered.

'Ten years is a long time. What if I studied twice as hard as all your other students?'

'Twenty years,' replied the master.

'Twenty years!' What if I practise unrelentingly, day and night with all my effort?'

'Thirty years,' replied the master.

'How is it that each time I say I will work harder you tell me that it will take longer?' the student asked, quite confused by now.

'The answer is clear,' said the master. 'When there is one eye fixed upon your destination, there is only one eye left with which to find your way.'*

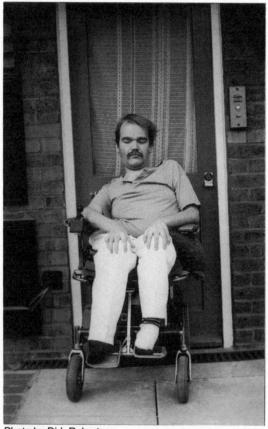 

Photo by Dirk Robertson

* An old Japanese story from: *Advanced Shotokan Karate Kata* by John Van Weenan (Paul Hooley Associates, 1987).

It is in the learning of the art and skill of meditation that many people who have varying degrees of difficulty in physical motor movements as well as learning difficulties can and do excel. Pushing the limitations of the mind to experience a feeling of 'nowness' and harmony with oneself and one's surroundings is of absolute benefit to people in general, and builds up a bank of credit on which you can draw at any time, once you have mastered the basics.

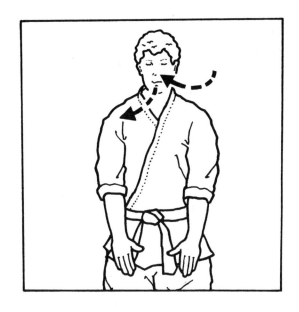

The deep breathing and relaxation exercise dates back to the Samurai (Japanese feudal period warriors) who sought a way to clear their minds before battle, even though death or serious injury might be waiting, or — even worse (for them) — possible dishonour by not performing their best.

When breathing patterns are combined with meditation, this exercise is known as *Moksu* and is widely practised by martial artists in order to 'unclutter' the mind and allow the mind and body to relax totally in order to perform to the maximum. Adopt the posture most comfortable for you. Breathe in through the nose and out through the mouth, as in the breathing pattern described in Part One.

If you are unable to see, close your eyes and rest your upper limbs, if you possess any, in front of you.

Breathe in through the nose and out through the mouth, pushing the breath as far down to the stomach as possible, expanding your stomach but keeping the chest still. When thoughts force their way into your mind, do not panic: just imagine them leaving as you breathe out. Do not force anything; just visualise calm and make your 'mind like water', still and calm, absorbing noise and external elements until peace is ultimately achieved.

POSTSCRIPT

I really enjoy my martial arts and hope that you find this book useful and informative. Years ago I read in a book that the author considered martial arts to have saved his life. I presumed that this meant he had used his skills to beat off assailants and save the day. Only now do I even begin to grasp what he meant. Peace of mind and a relaxed, fluid attitude to life and all its problems seem like a saviour to me.

In conclusion, I use the term which will be extremely familiar to many martial artists and those of you who have come across Zen. It is an over-used phrase — but it's still the best for me:

'Better to light a candle than to complain of the dark.'

DIRK ROBERTSON
London 1991

APPENDICES

COACHING PEOPLE WITH SPECIAL NEEDS

The coaching of individuals in any activity requires a sound knowledge of their needs, requirements and ability to understand the information being imparted in a given fashion. Thus if someone with hearing difficulties is the recipient of information which is delivered verbally, any difficulties which he or she may have probably relate not to the material but to the *way* in which it is being taught.

This must always be taken into account when instructing people with any type of disability. If you are a teacher, do not be afraid to ask someone what method of tuition he or she finds most comfortable. Do not presume that people are incapable of learning or lacking in interest just because they do not seem to be picking things up as fast as others. If there is a problem, most people will tell you — IF YOU ASK THEM!

People with disabilities are no different from anyone else. When they come to a class, in martial arts or any other activity, they come to learn, to enjoy themselves and, if only temporarily, to leave the problems of the world behind.

Whilst it is important to be sensitive to their particular situation, their disability should not be the central focus all the time. Their *ability* to learn, listen and adapt should be built

Members of the British Squad at the World Judo Championships for Blind People in Holland in July 1990, with Team Coach Steve Pullen (*far left*) and Team Manager Eileen Cartmell (*far right*).

on and encouraged. Do not be over-protective or an instant expert on people with disabilities. The experts are the people themselves, so listen to what they have to say.

I accompanied a little girl, who has no arms, to a Karate class where everyone else was able-bodied. After the initial curiosity and overlong stares (which she handled herself) she joined in the class and was able to demonstrate her ability to learn and to show others her particular strengths — such as co-ordination and dramatic flexibility of her lower limbs. She enjoyed herself and appeared to be a part of the whole activity. This is the key to successful coaching and instruction of people, whether they have disabilities or not.

If you run a martial arts class, contact the Local Authority to let them know that people with disabilities are welcome, and ensure that the centre where you teach is aware of your declaration of integration. If you are uncertain how to proceed, contact one of the addresses at the end of the book, where you can get advice and support as well as information related specifically to people with special needs.

The Judo section of the British Blind Sport Association concentrates firmly on integration of sighted and non-sighted participants. Visually impaired people are seen as ideal competitors since Judo is a tactile sport which, according to the publicity material of the Association, you could do 'blindfold'. In competition there are weight categories, so people are equally matched. In training, at clubs, everybody trains together although juniors and seniors are normally separated, so again, there is not much chance of being out of your depth!

There is much debate about whether Judo is or is not a martial art. In its present form it is a sport but its roots, both in terms of technique and philosophy, lie firmly in the martial traditions and it is clearly an excellent activity both for sighted people and for people who are visually impaired.

WORLD JUDO CHAMPIONSHIPS FOR BLIND PEOPLE
Assen, Holland, July 1990

RESULTS

Country	Gold	Silver	Bronze	Position
Gt. Britain	2	—	3	1st
Russia	1 + 1	2		2nd
France	1	1	1	3rd
USA	1	1		4th
Australia	1			5th
Spain		1 + 1	3	6th
Korea		1		7th
Italy			2	(joint) 8th
Belgium			1	9th
Canada				10th

+ 1 = Unofficial medal, below minimum number of competitors in that category.
Elieen Cartmell (*Team Manager*)   Simon Shorrick (*Publicity Officer*)

Photo by David Bruce

GLOSSARY

Age Uke. Rising block.

Age Zuki. Rising punch.

Aikido. Fighting art with emphasis on fluid movements and 'giving' to an opponent's strength, thus turning it on one's attacker.

Bassai-Dai. Karate Kata of the Shotokan style, meaning to 'storm a fortress'.

Bodhidharma. Indian monk said to be the originator of martial arts.

Budo-Bushido. Way of the warrior.

Chinte. Kata — Chinese origin.

Choku Zuki. Straight punch.

Chudan. Middle level.

Confucius. Chinese philosopher.

Dachi. Stance.

Dan. Black Belt grade.

Do. Way.

Dojo. Training hall — the way place.

Empi. 'Flight of Swallows' Kata.

Enpi. Elbow.

Enpi Uchi. Elbow strike.

Enpi Uke. Elbow block.

Forms. Series of postures from Tai-Chi-Chuan and other martial arts.

Fudo-Dachi. Modification of the front stance.

Gedan. Lower level.

Gedan Zuki. Lower punch.

Geri. Kick.

Gi. Training suit.

Gichin Funakoshi. Originator of modern Karate.

Goju-Ryu. 'Hard-soft' style of Okinawan Karate.

Gung-Fu. Former name for 'Kung-Fu'.

Gyaku Zuki. Reverse punch.

Hachiji-Dachi. Natural open-leg stance.

Haishu Uchi. Back of the hand strike.

Haishu Uke. Back of the hand block.

Haitō Uchi. Ridge hand strike.

Haitō Uke. Ridge hand block.

Haiwan. Back of arms.

Hara. Spirit, supposed to be just below the stomach.

Heisoku-Dachi. Informal attention stance when performing a bow.

Hiza. Knee.

Hiza Geri. Knee kick.

I Ching. Book of changes. Philosophical book.

Ippon. Full point in competition Karate and other martial arts.

Jitte. Traditional Kata.

Jodan. Upper level.

Judo. Japanese traditional 'sport' and art with emphasis on throws.

Juji Uke. X block.

Kage Uke. Hooking block.

Kage Zuki. Hooking punch.

Kakato. Heel.

Kakiwaki Uke. Wedge block.

Kanku-Dai. 'To look at the sky' — Shotokan Karate.

Karate. Empty hand Japanese fighting art.

Kata. Set series of formal exercises.

Keito Uke. Chicken head wrist block.

Kendo. Way of the sword.

Ki. Spirit.

Kiba Dachi. Straddle or horse stance.

Kiai. Shout used to unite spirit and body.

Kime. Focus.

Kizami Zuki. Snap punch.

Kokutsu-Dachi. Back stance.

Kokyo. Breathing.

Kumite. Sparring.

Kun. Oath.

Kyu. Junior grade.

Kyokushinkai. 'Ultimate Truth'. Hard, tough traditional style of Karate, very popular.

Lao Tze. Chinese philosopher.

Mae Geri. Front kick.

Mawashi Zuki. Round house punch.

Mawate. Turn.

Moksu. Meditation.

Morehei Uyeshiba. Originator of Aikido.

Morote Uke. Augmented block.

Morote Zuki. Augmented punch.

Nekoashi-Dachi. Cat stance.

Oi Zuki. Lunge punch.

Okinawa. Island off the mainland of Japan.

Rei. Bow.

Seiza. Kneeling position.

Sensei. Teacher.

Shoto. Funakoshi's pen-name.

Shao-Lin. Monastery.

Shutō Uchi. Knife hand strike.

Shutō Uke. Knife hand block.

Shotokan. Style of Japanese Karate with emphasis on low, strong techniques.

Shukokai. Style of Karate with emphasis on double hip movement.

Soto Ude Uke. Outside forearm block.

Taekwondo. Korean martial art.

Tai-Chi-Chuan. Martial form of Chinese origin.

Tao Te Ching. Famous work promoting specific philosophy.

Taoism. Eastern philosophy.

Tate Zuki. Vertical fist punch.

Teisho Uchi. Palm heel strike.

Tettsui Uchi. Bottom fist strike.

Tobi-Geri. Jumping kick.

Tsuki. Punching.

Uchi. Strike.

Uchi Ude Uke. Inside block.

Uke. Block.

Unsu. 'Cloud hands' Kata.

Ura Zuki. Close punch.

Ushiro Geri. Back kick.

Ushiro Mawashi Geri. Reverse roundhouse kick.

Wado-Ryu. Style of Karate. *Ryu* means 'school', 'way of peace'.

Wazari. Half-point in competition Karate and other martial arts.

Wushu. Believed to be the correct name for 'Kung-Fu' — Chinese martial acrobatics and weapon techniques.

Wu-Tang. Mountain in China.

Yama Zuki. U punch.

Yame. Stop.

Yoko Enpi Uchi. Side elbow strike.

Yoko Geri. Side kick.

Zenkutsu-Dachi. Front stance.

Zuki. Punch.

USEFUL ADDRESSES

Magazines

Combat (Ed. Paul Clifton), 135 Aldridge Road, Perry Barr, Birmingham B42 2ET.

Fighting Arts International (Ed. Terry O'Neill), PO Box 26, Birkenhead, Merseyside, L43 4YQ.

Martial Arts Illustrated (Ed. Bob Sykes), Revenue Chambers, St Peter's Street, Huddersfield, West Yorkshire, HD1 1DL.

Shotokan Karate Magazine (Ed. John Cheetham), 1 Grove Court, Lymm, Cheshire.

American Karate (Ed. David Weiss), 351 West 54th Street, New York, NY 10019, U.S.A.

Associations and Groups

British Blind Sport Association, Heygates Lodge, Elkington, Northampton, NN6 7NH.

British Sport Association for Disabled People, Mary Glen Haig Suite, 31 Osnaburgh Street, London NW 1 3ND.

Federation of Shotokan Karate, PO Box 47, West PDO, Nottingham, NG8 2EA.

Martial Arts Commission, 1st Floor, 15–16 Deptford Broadway, London SE8 4PE.

The National Coaching Foundation, 4 College Close, Beckett Park, Leeds, LS6 3QH.

The Sports Council, 16 Upper Woburn Place, London WC1 OQP.

United Kingdom Sports Association for People with a Mental Handicap, 30 Phillip Lane, Tottenham, London N15 4JD.